People of Destiny

A Humanities Series

There comes a time,
we know not when,
that marks
the destiny of men.

Joseph Addison Alexander

People of Destiny

ALBERT SCHWEITZER

By Kenneth G. Richards

CHILDRENS PRESS, CHICAGO

*The editors wish to express
their appreciation to Mr. Meyer Goldberg,
who created the series and inspired
the publication of* People of Destiny.

Cover and body design: John Hollis

Project editor: Joan Downing

Editorial assistant: Gerri Stoller

*Illustrations: Bob Brunton—Hollis
Associates*

Research editor: Robert Hendrickson

*Photographs: From the files of Wide
World Photos, Inc.*

Typesetting: American Typesetting Co.

Printing: The Regensteiner Corporation

Quotations on pages 10; 25, col. 1; and 32, ll. 25-36 from The Three
Worlds of Albert Schweitzer *by Robert Payne, ©1957 Robert
Payne, Published by Thomas Nelson & Sons.*

*Quotations on pages 13, 38, 43, 44, 49, 52, 53, 55, 58, 61, 63, 66,
and 68 from* Out of My Life and Thought *by Albert Schweitzer.
Translated by C. T. Campion. Copyright 1933, 1949, ©1961 by
Holt, Rinehart and Winston, Inc. Reprinted by permission of Holt,
Rinehart and Winston, Inc. and George Allen & Unwin Ltd.,
London.*

*Quotations on pages 18; 19; 21; 22; 23; 25, col. 2; 27; 28; 29; 31;
32, ll. 6-16; and 35 from* Memoirs of Childhood and Youth *by
Albert Schweitzer. Reprinted by permission of George Allen &
Unwin Ltd., London.*

2 3 4 5 6 7 8 9 10 11 12 13 14 15 16 17 18 19 20 21 22 23 24 25 R 75 74 73 72 71 70 69

Contents

Destination Lambaréné

On April 14, 1913, the steamer *Europe* anchored off Cape Lopez on the coast of French Equatorial Africa. From the deck of the ship, a tall man with a bristling mustache stared at the strangely beautiful land he was seeing for the first time. At his side, his wife shielded her eyes from the blistering glare of the tropical sun, and together they studied their awesome new environment. Here at the mouth of the mighty Ogowe River, the dark, steaming, virgin jungle rose in forbidding majesty at the water's edge. Some 250 miles ahead, in the midst of this primeval forest, lay the destination of Dr. Albert Schweitzer and his wife Helene. It was a place called Lambaréné.

As the couple watched, a white stern-wheeler riverboat appeared as if by magic from the dark green maze of the jungle shoreline. With its stack belching black smoke and its paddle wheel churning the murky water, the steamer *Alembe* slowly made its way alongside the larger ocean vessel. After watching their seventy cases of medical supplies safely transferred to the riverboat, Schweitzer and his wife stepped aboard the *Alembe* to begin the next leg of their journey. At last, with a clang of bells and a toot of the whistle, the little paddle-wheeler pulled away from the *Europe* and pointed its bow up the Ogowe. In a little while, the ocean was lost from view and the boat and its passengers were swallowed up by the surrounding jungle.

For the first few hundred miles from the ocean, the Ogowe is more a river system than a single definable stream.

*"We seemed to be dreaming . . .
an ancient landscape, which elsewhere
seemed but the creation of man's fancy,
had suddenly sprung to life . . ."*

It is a sluggish expanse of yellow, brackish water which sprawls across the area like a giant creeping vine. Dr. Schweitzer later described his first impressions of the area in a book:

"We seemed to be dreaming. An ancient landscape, which elsewhere had seemed but the creation of man's fancy, had suddenly sprung to life. Impossible to say where the river ends and the land begins. A vast tangle of roots clothed in lianas rose fron the water. Palm shrubs and palm trees, and among them other trees with green boughs and powerful branches and leaves, and standing among them trees towering heavenward, and vast fields of papyrus as high as a man with giant fan-shaped leaves, and in all this lush greenness, dead giants with decayed branches pointing high in the sky. Every gap in the forest revealed a blinding mirror of water, and with every bend of the river another branch of the river came in sight."

Throughout the long, hot afternoon, the *Alembe* chugged steadily up the river. Once they stopped at a native village where workers brought some three thousand logs aboard for the wood-burning engine. When the tropical night descended, the little boat plodded on in the ghostly darkness as stars twinkled above and lightning flashed on the horizon. On this, his first night in Africa, Dr. Schweitzer slipped under his mosquito netting and tried in vain to sleep.

With each turn of the paddle wheel he was nearing his destination and his long-sought destiny. Behind lay civilization, good friends, fame, position, culture, and security. Ahead lay filth, pain, disease, deprivation, and ignorance. But Dr. Schweitzer held no doubts as to the rightfulness of his chosen life. It was not an impromptu decision which brought him to Africa. He was here after years of preparation during which he never once lost sight of his goal.

As the *Alembe* chugged steadily through the eerie darkness of the Ogowe, Dr. Schweitzer reflected upon those years of toil and dedication which had led so inexorably to this time and this place. It had really begun some

On an April day in 1913, Dr. Albert Schweitzer and his wife Helene left the steamer Europe *at Cape Lopez on the coast of French Equatorial Africa. They boarded the white stern-wheeler riverboat* Alembe *(left) for the long hot ride up the Ogowe River to Lambaréné, where the doctor planned to start a jungle hospital.*

seventeen years before when he was twenty-one. One bright morning in his home at Günsbach he had made a promise to dedicate himself to the service of humanity. The vow was made in response to a saying of Jesus: "Whosoever shall lose his life for My sake shall save it." His plan allowed himself nine years—until he was thirty—for study and learning and for his musical career. After that he would give his life to serving his fellowmen.

The nine years had been filled with achievement. Degrees in philosophy and theology were followed by a professorship at the University of Strasbourg. He also drew fame as an author and as one of the greatest organists in all Europe. But the call of destiny was not heard until the autumn of 1904 when he was twenty-nine years old.

With only a year remaining of his self-allotted period of preparation, Schweitzer happened, one day, to glance at the magazine of the Paris Missionary Society. As he sat, idly turning the pages, his eyes fell on the title of an article by the president of the Society,

"The Needs of the Congo Mission." It was a plea for Christian workers to offer their services to help alleviate the terrible suffering of the natives in the Gabon section of the Congo Colony. It was a brief article, but as Schweitzer reported later, "The article finished, I quietly began my work. My search was over."

How best to serve the Africans became the big question in the mind of Albert Schweitzer. He soon realized that what they needed most were doctors. And so, despite attempts by friends to dissuade him, Schweitzer embarked on a seven-year course of medical study. In February of 1913, he received his medical degree and, within a month, had begun the journey which brought him to this night on the Ogowe River.

Morning dawned hot and still. The only motion of the humid jungle air was caused by the movement of the *Alembe* as it moved farther and farther into the Dark Continent. It was late in the morning when the steamer arrived at Lambaréné. Waiting to greet the *Alembe* were several native dugout canoes. After much hard work, the packing cases of supplies were transferred to the canoes and then Dr. Schweitzer and his wife bid goodby to the *Alembe's* captain and slipped into a native boat.

With the native oarsmen standing and singing as they paddled, the canoes sliced gracefully through the water for nearly half an hour. As Schweitzer and his wife peered anxiously ahead, the boats turned into a smaller side-stream, and for the first time came in sight of the mission station of Lambaréné.

Dr. Schweitzer had expected a small settlement, but found instead that the mission consisted of only a few tumble-down buildings situated on three low hills. The dense and ominous jungle stood menacingly only twenty yards away. It was nearly dark when the Schweitzers stepped ashore, their long journey at last ended.

Weak and exhausted, the weary couple trudged to the top of a hill where their new home awaited, It was a small four-room house on stilts with bare, crumbling walls and was infested with spiders and cockroaches. The conditions were enough to shatter the determination of all but the bravest heart.

When finally Dr. Schweitzer tumbled into bed, he lay awake for a long while listening to the sounds of the African night. Mosquitos buzzed incessantly around his bed and cockroaches scratched across the bare floors. Outside, crickets chirped in the clearing and strange birds screeched in the tangled jungle beyond. Hippos moved ponderously about in nearby swamps and crocodiles slithered along the banks

When the Alembe *reached Lambaréné, it was met by several native dugout canoes. After the supplies had been transferred from the* Alembe, *Dr. Schweitzer and his wife bid good-bye to the captain and got into one of the canoes. With the native oarsmen standing and singing as they paddled, the canoes sliced gracefully through the water (left). Nearly half an hour later, the boats turned into a smaller side-stream and Dr. Schweitzer and his wife caught their first glimpse of the mission station of Lambaréné.*

13

...the weeks would stretch into years and the years into decades of sacrifice, toil, and service to humanity...

of the Ogowe. Through the night, jungle drums throbbed a message to distant ears. It was quite late when sleep came at last to Dr. Schweitzer.

Morning came early to the jungle clearing and with it the ever-oppressive heat and humidity. Dr. Schweitzer arose and stepped out on the porch of his bungalow where a strange spectacle awaited him. It was a sight he would grow accustomed to in the days ahead. Below the porch steps crouched and squatted a circle of natives who greeted him with silent, pleading stares. Word of his coming had spread through the district like wildfire. Throughout the night, the sick had hobbled or were carried along jungle trails or were whisked over the winding river in their hollowed-log canoes. Now they watched him in their hopeless, uncomplaining way—suffering in quiet resignation.

The doctor stared briefly at the silent crowd below him. These people were his reason for coming to this primitive land. In a moment he descended the steps and began to administer to the first of his African patients.

This was to be Dr. Albert Schweitzer's destiny. Beginning on this April day in 1913, the weeks would stretch into years and the years into decades of sacrifice, toil, and service to humanity. In the end, this work at Lambaréné on the edge of the African jungle would stand as an everlasting monument to the finest principles of man's kindness and service to his fellowman.

Word of Dr. Schweitzer's coming had spread through the district like wildfire. Throughout the night, the sick had hobbled or had been carried through the jungle. When Dr. Schweitzer arose the following morning and stepped out onto the porch of his bungalow (below), he was greeted by a silent crowd of people who gazed at him with pleading stares. A moment later, he descended the steps and began to administer to the needs of his first African patients.

15

Boy of the Vosges

Alsace, with its sister region Lorraine, occupies the northeast corner of France, the border area of France and Germany. Throughout history these two great nations have battled over this region of vineyards and ancient castles. In 1871, following the Franco–Prussian War, the area was ceded to Germany and peace came once more to the Vosges Mountains. Four years later the area celebrated a fine vintage of grapes. Of lesser note in that year of 1875 was a birth in the ancient and once proud city of Kaysersberg. Though the birth went largely unnoticed at the time, the life that began on January 14, 1875, would be remembered by an admiring world in future years. On that day, in the Protestant manse, or parsonage, at Kaysersberg, Albert Schweitzer was born.

Albert was the second child and first son of Pastor Louis Schweitzer and his wife, Adele. On both sides of the family, Albert derived from solid old Alsatian stock. His paternal grandfather was a schoolmaster in Pfaffenhofen as were three great-uncles. His mother's father was the Pastor of Muhlbach in the Munster Valley of Alsace. He was named for his mother's half-brother, Pastor Albert Schillinger of Strasbourg. Thus, young Albert's roots lay deep in the rugged hills and valleys of the Vosges.

For the first few months of life, Albert Schweitzer hovered close to death. He was a sickly child from birth, with a sallow complexion and large grey eyes. Doctors could find no cure for the baby, who seemed to suffer constantly from fevers. Then, when Albert was six months old, his father moved the family to Günsbach, a small village some fifteen miles from Kaysersberg. The baby, in his mother's arms, attended the offi-

---

Albert Schweitzer, the second child of Pastor Louis Schweitzer and his wife Adele, was born on January 14, 1875, in Kaysersberg, Alsace, in the northeast corner of France. Throughout history, France and Germany have battled over this border region of vineyards and castles (left).

cial installation of his father as pastor of the church. He has described the occasion in a book:

"My mother had decked me out as finely as she could in a white frock with colored ribbons, but not one of the pastor's wives who had come to the ceremony ventured to compliment her on her thin and yellow-faced baby, and none of them went beyond embarrassed commonplaces. So at last my mother—she has often told me about it—could restrain herself no longer: she fled with me in her arms to her bedroom, and there wept hot tears over me."

Even as the townspeople whispered that the new pastor's first funeral would be that of his son, Mrs. Schweitzer was determined to save her child. Her care and prayers and "milk from neighbor Leopold's cow, together with the excel-lent Günsbach air, worked wonders for me; from my second year onward I improved marvelously, and became a strong and healthy boy."

Günsbach is a lovely little village nestled among the vineyards of the Munster Valley. Fruit trees send forth scent from their blossoms in the spring air and the surrounding hills are heavily forested with beech and pine. Goats and cows roam the pastured slopes above the church steeple. This beautiful pastoral setting was to be Albert Schweitzer's home for the first nine years of his life.

Albert Schweitzer's first recollection was of "seeing the devil." Each Sunday at church, the shaggy face of the "devil" would appear during the services staring down at the congregation from within a frame near the organ. Young Albert, who was only three or four years old,

When Albert was six months old, his father became pastor of the church in Günsbach, a village about fifteen miles from Kayserberg. Albert's first childhood recollection was of "seeing the face of the devil" during Sunday church services in Günsbach. The face appeared to be staring down from within a frame near the organ (above). When he was older, Albert realized the face he saw was that of the organist, reflected in a mirror above the organ.

was transfixed by this apparition. It appeared only during the singing and playing but disappeared as soon as his father began his sermon. "This is the devil that is looking down into the church," young Albert reasoned, "but as soon as father begins with God's Word, he has to make himself scarce!" In time, Albert came to understand that the face he saw was that of "Daddy" Iltis, the organist, reflected in a mirror above the organ. Of course, he did not play while Pastor Schweitzer was praying at the altar, which explained his disappearance at that time. "This weekly dose of visible theology gave quite a distinctive tone to my childish piety," Albert remembered with a smile in later years.

Though the "devil" in the church was purely imaginary, young Albert

soon encountered another more human devil in the form of Jaegle, the grave-digger and church sacristan. This rather malevolent old man became what Albert later called "the terror of my childhood." Each Sunday morning, Jaegle would appear at the door to learn the numbers of the hymns to be sung at church. It was Albert's job to pass this information on and he soon came to dread this weekly meeting with the gnarled old man. Jaegle had convinced the boy that he would soon grow horns on his head and each Sunday he would grasp the boy's forehead and say, "Yes, the horns are growing!" After a year of this mental torture, Pastor Schweitzer managed to convince his son that no man could grow horns.

Another time, old Jaegle told the boy that when he was conscripted for military service in the Prussian army he would have to be fitted for a suit of iron clothes. The thought haunted young Albert, and for days he waited in front of the village blacksmith shop waiting to see soldiers come to be measured for their iron suits. It was some time later that his mother explained to him that soldiers wore cloth uniforms.

The early years were pleasant ones for Albert. There was little money for anything except the necessities of life. The small stipend of a village pastor did not allow for any luxuries. Still, Mrs. Schweitzer managed to feed her happy family, which soon consisted of five children. Besides Albert and his elder sister, Louise, there were sisters Adele and Margerit, and little brother Paul. A sixth child, named Emma, died in infancy. Albert's father was a somewhat remote figure during these early years. Most of his time was spent in his small study, which was cluttered with musty books. Though frequently plagued with illness, Pastor Schweitzer lived to a ripe old age.

On warm summer days the family would pack a picnic lunch and climb the slopes of the surrounding hills to the deep forests above the village. The hours spent in these quiet forests were among the most pleasant in the young life of Albert Schweitzer. He soon developed a deep love for nature. As he grew a little older he would spend many hours in quiet solitude among the craggy hills and bubbling mountain streams.

At last Albert came of school age and one fine October day his father took him off to the village school. Like many a new first grader, Albert cried all the way. "I suspected that an end had now come to my dreams and my glorious freedom," Albert remembered later. But he carried his dreaming with him into the schoolroom and throughout his early schooling was not a particularly good student.

Albert, however, had a natural ear for music. Even before entering school, his father had started giving him les-

Albert's early years were pleasant ones. The five children and their parents often packed a picnic lunch on warm summer days and climbed the slopes of the surrounding hills to the deep forests above the village of Günsbach (opposite). The boy soon developed a deep love for nature and as he grew older, spent many hours among the hills and mountain streams.

sons on the old square piano the family had inherited from Grandfather Schillinger. His ability on the piano proved a happy surprise to his schoolteacher who could only peck out tunes with one finger.

Though at this early age Albert's musical ability was somewhat limited, he nonetheless had a deep feeling for harmony. In later years he recalled the first time he had heard the blending of human voices in song. "The charm of the two-part harmony of the songs thrilled me all over, to my very marrow, and, similarly, the first time I heard brass instruments playing together I almost fainted from excess of pleasure."

The discoveries in harmony added new depth to Albert's love of music, and he practiced more determinedly than ever. With his new zeal he proved an apt musician. By the time he was seven he was composing his own hymns. Soon he was playing the church organ, though his feet could hardly reach the pedals.

And so the early years passed pleasantly for young Albert Schweitzer. It was an era of peace in central Europe, and Alsace was now a part of the mighty new German Empire under the leadership of the great Bismarck. German was the official language and Pastor Schweitzer delivered his sermons in German. At home, however, the Alsatian dialect was spoken, which is a blending of German and French. Of course, the family could speak French as well as German and Alsatian, and this was the language in which they always wrote their letters.

These quiet formative years in Günsbach had a profound influence upon the emerging character of Albert Schweitzer. Through his love of animals, he developed an acute sensitivity to pain. A limping horse, an injured dog, or a dying bird all raised in him the burning question of why so many living creatures had to suffer pain. He wondered why prayers were offered only for human beings. "So when my mother had prayed with me and had kissed me good night, I used to add silently a prayer that I had composed myself for all living creatures. It ran thus: 'O heavenly Father, protect and bless all things that have breath; guard them all from evil, and let them sleep in peace.'"

Religion was, of course, a big part of Albert Schweitzer's early life. When he was eight, his father gave him a New Testament, which the boy read eagerly. But it seemed that many questions that Albert raised on the subject were unanswerable. "What did the parents of Jesus do, I asked myself, with the gold and other valuables which they got from the three Wise Men? How could they be so poor after that? And that the Wise Men should never have troubled themselves again about the Child Jesus was to me incomprehensible." His search for the answers to these and other questions would result in his great work of later years called "The Quest for the Historical Jesus."

There were other influences that would direct the destiny of Albert Schweitzer. From the pulpit, his father often delivered sermons on the subject

of missionary work. Pastor Schweitzer admired an obscure missionary named Casalis who wrote numerous letters from his missionary station in Africa. Albert was enthralled by the accounts of the great humanitarian work amid the jungles of the Dark Continent.

One summer on a visit to Colmar, the capital of Alsace, Albert visited the gardens of *Champs de Mars* and the great statue of Admiral Bruat. At the base of the statue were four carved figures representing the four corners of the earth. Africa, or the south, was represented by a giant Negro, his head bowed yet noble as if he proudly bore a world of grief. This statue was by Auguste Bartholdi, a fellow Alsatian who, even as Albert gazed upon the giant Negro, was busy completing his greatest work—the Statue of Liberty. The handsome Negro made a profound impression on Albert. In later years, he would remember, "It was this statue by Bartholdi which summoned me at the age of thirty to live and work in Africa."

In 1884, when Albert was nine, he was sent to attend the *Realschule*, a secondary school at Munster some two miles down the valley. From that fall, through the harsh Alsatian winter and into following spring, young Albert walked the two miles to and from school each day. In fact, it was these lonely walks that he enjoyed most about this school year. He disliked most of his subjects, except history, and consequently his grades suffered.

Albert was a sensitive boy at this stage of his life. Rather shy and introverted, he nevertheless was liked by his classmates and they played together during recess time. He took all games quite seriously and this led at times to a display of his very quick temper. This characteristic he inherited from his mother and also his maternal grandfather Schillinger. "I began to feel anxious about my passion for play, and gradually gave up all games," Albert remembered later. "I have never ventured to touch a playing card."

As the school year ended in the early summer of 1885, Albert's family was disturbed by his rather poor grades. As they considered what to do with the boy, an offer came from Albert's Uncle Louis who was director of the Mulhausen primary schools. Mulhausen, or Mulhouse, is an industrial city in Alsace and, being two hours away from Günsbach by train, Albert's enrollment at the Gymnasium (secondary school) required that he go there to live with his Great-uncle Louis and Great-aunt Sophie. These, his godparents, offered to support the boy, free of charge, and Albert's parents quickly and gratefully accepted the offer.

And so, in the autumn of 1885, young Albert Schweitzer left his quiet home in Günsbach and made the journey to Mulhouse where he was destined to attend school for the next eight years. This was the first important milestone in the remarkable life of Albert Schweitzer.

Religion, of course, was a big part of Albert's early life, and when he was eight, his father gave him a New Testament, which the boy read eagerly. But it seemed that many questions Albert raised on the subject were unanswerable. His search for the answers to these and other questions would result in his great work of later years called "The Quest for the Historical Jesus." Opposite, Albert gazes up at a statue of the one who prompted his questions.

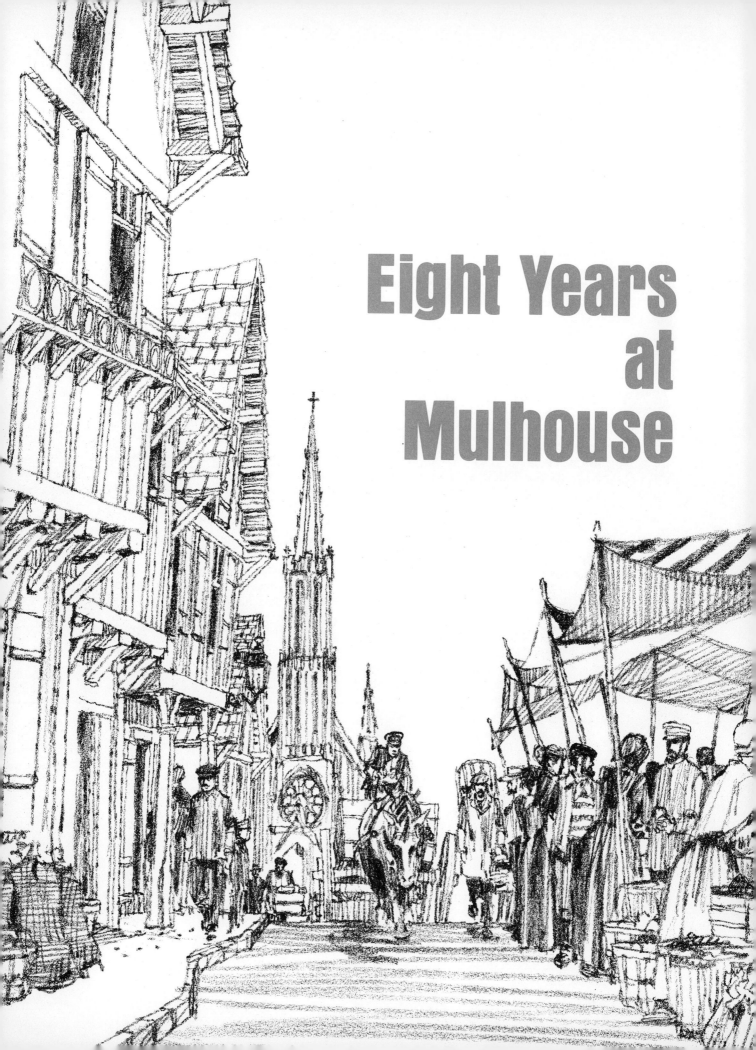

Eight Years at Mulhouse

Life at Mulhouse began badly for Albert Schweitzer. He did not like the city at first and missed the quiet pastoral setting of his early childhood. Uncle Louis and Aunt Sophie were childless, and Albert missed the happy companionship of his brother and sisters. The uncomfortable apartment within the school building was cold and clammy, as were the classrooms themselves. But Albert suffered in silence and, in time, came to accept his fate philosophically.

His aunt and uncle were stern disciplinarians and their whole lives were governed by the clock. Every hour was allocated to certain specific daily activities and functions. For Albert, certain times were set aside for piano lessons and practice, for homework, and for reading. Aunt Sophie attached great importance to being punctual and obedient. She also insisted that Albert always pay attention to his elders, be seen and not heard, and keep himself clean at all times. Aunt Sophie discouraged any forwardness on the part of the boy in her belief that reserve was the essence of good breeding. "As time went on," Albert wrote in later life, "I ventured to emancipate myself somewhat from these rules about well-bred reserve."

There was little fun or enjoyment in this strictly regimented household. "Sunday was the only time that was really devoted to recreation," Schweitzer remembered later. "Then we went for a walk, and after that I had till ten o'clock to gratify my passion for reading." Aunt Sophie found reason to complain about his reading habits. She detested the way he "devoured" books. He read much too rapidly, she said, to enjoy the style. This she considered most important. Albert soon learned that "it was necessary to avoid irritating her on the reading question."

Young Albert liked to read the newspapers but his aunt accused him of reading only the murder cases. "She did her best to get my newspaper reading prohibited," he recalled. Eleven-year-old Albert tried to explain that he was interested mainly in politics and contemporary history. He was aware that Grover Cleveland was the President of the United States; he was following with interest the exploration of Greenland by such men as Robert E. Peary; and he knew of the annexation by Germany of the Marshall and Solomon Islands in the Pacific. He had a broad interest in many happenings the world over. But his godparents decided to test him. "Who are the ruling princes in the Balkan States?" they asked. "What was the composition of the last three French cabinets?" Albert was up to the test. "I came through with flying colors," he wrote later, "and thereupon the decision was given that I might read the papers."

Strict requirements were laid down for his practice on the piano. This had the effect of making what had once been a pleasure a chore. As a result, he tended to improvise instead of learning to play properly. His music master, Eugen Munch, almost despaired of him. One day, in exasperation, Munch cried, "Really you don't deserve to have such

In 1885, Albert Schweitzer went to Mulhouse (opposite) to live with his uncle and aunt, both of whom were very strict with Albert. He attended the Gymnasium (secondary school) there for the next eight years.

beautiful music given you to play. If a boy has no feeling, I certainly can't give him any!"

"Oho," Schweitzer thought to himself, "I'll show you whether I have any feeling or not!" Then he went home to practice diligently for a whole week, determined to prove himself. He experimented with the fingering, found the best and wrote it above the notes of his music sheets. The next time he played for Munch he poured his heart and soul into a rendition of *Lied ohne Worte* by Mendelssohn. The master listened with awe to Albert's playing, so moved that he could only press the boy's shoulders in a gesture of pride and appreciation when the piece was finished. After that, Albert progressed through Beethoven and then to Bach.

At the end of the school year, in the spring of 1886, Albert returned home with a report card so bad that there was doubt whether he would be allowed to continue in school. His parents did not scold him but he was deeply aware of their concern. He noticed that his mother's eyes were red from weeping and he promised himself to try harder in the coming year. He was also reminded that he would have only one last chance.

For awhile during the next school year he reverted once more to his old habit of daydreaming in class. And then one day a new teacher arrived by the name of Dr. Wehmann. Albert noticed with fascination how very carefully Dr. Wehmann prepared and delivered each lesson he gave. To the boy, this teacher became a "model of fulfillment of duty." Albert decided to conduct his studies in the same precise manner that Dr. Wehmann prepared his lessons. The results were amazing, to say the least, to both his parents and his teachers. Within three months Albert's grades were high enough to place him near the top of the class. This trait of seeing each task through to its completion, with care and exactness, was to stay with Albert Schweitzer all the rest of his life.

Henceforth, Albert took a genuine interest in his studies and applied himself to them with great diligence.

During Albert's first school year at the Gymnasium in Mulhouse, he spent so much of his time day-dreaming that his grades were very bad. The following year, he had a teacher who prepared his lessons very carefully. This teacher, Dr. Wehmann, was to become a model for Albert to follow. He decided to conduct his studies in the same precise manner in which Dr. Wehmann prepared the class lessons. The results were amazing; Albert's grades went up and he began to take a genuine interest in his studies. History was his best subject; next to that he enjoyed science most. Above, he conducts a science experiment.

Throughout the rest of his years at the Gymnasium at Mulhouse, history was his best subject, and he mastered the course with little effort. He would later attribute this to his passion for reading, which by now was concentrated on works of history. Next to history he enjoyed science most. Yet he could never be satisfied with the simple little textbook explanations of the workings of nature. On his lonely walks in the valley of Munster, he had observed first-hand the special grandeur of clouds and lightning and all the many other mysteries of nature. "It became clear to me that what we label Force or 'Life' remains in its own essential nature forever inexplicable."

Literature and mathematics were Albert's weak points, although he managed to get respectable grades through hard work and study. He especially disliked having poetry and the classics explained to him. Poems, he believed, should be felt and experienced—not dissected and examined like a biology subject. He grew to dislike Homer intensely

when he was made to learn the relationships of all the heroes, gods, and goddesses that appeared in Homer's poems.

Each summer, Albert returned to Günsbach and the family home. These were joyous months for the boy. In 1889, the family came into a small inheritance from a distant relative. Also they were supplied with a new house, larger and more comfortable than the older one. It was about this time, too, that Pastor Schweitzer's health began to improve. During these happy years, father and son drew closer to one another and a warm companionship developed.

The year 1890 saw the resignation of Chancellor Bismarck at the insistence of William II, now in the second year of his reign. The young and charming emperor, better known as Kaiser Wilhelm, would eventually lead his country into world war and ruin. But as the last decade of the nineteenth century dawned, Germany was at peace and Albert Schweitzer pursued his education with little concern for future events.

Albert turned fifteen in this year of 1890, and it was at this time that he began to make great strides in his musical career. His tutor, Eugen Munch, began giving Albert lessons on the beautiful great organ at St. Stephen's Church in Mulhouse. Albert had done well on the old organ in his father's church at Günsbach where he often substituted for the aging "Daddy" Iltis. The great organ at Mulhouse was much more complicated, however, and had three keyboards and sixty-two stops. By now Munch recognized the great potential of young Albert and the boy had nothing but admiration for the great organist.

Within a year, when Albert was only sixteen, he was allowed to take the place of his tutor during church services. Soon afterward, he played his first concert with the church choir. Albert provided the organ accompaniment of Brahms' *Requiem*. It was a great thrill for the young musician and a moment he would remember and treasure all his life. "For the first time," he would remember, "I knew the joy, which I have so often tasted since then, of letting the organ send the flood of its own special tones to mingle with the music of choir and orchestra."

During his stay at Mulhouse, Albert was sent to special classes to prepare for confirmation. Here he came under the tutelage of Pastor Wennagel, for whom he had great respect. Albert differed, however, with the pastor's basic precepts. Pastor Wennagel wanted his charge to silence all reasoning in deference to blind faith. "But I was convinced," wrote Schweitzer later, "and I am so still—that the fundamental principles of Christianity have to be

When Albert was fifteen, his music teacher began giving him lessons on the beautiful organ at St. Stephen's Church in Mulhouse (opposite). This great organ was much more complicated than the one Albert had played at his father's church in Günsbach, and had three keyboards and sixty-two stops. Within a year, Albert's musical accomplishments were such that he was often allowed to take the place of his tutor during church services and soon he played his first concert with the church choir.

proved by reasoning, and by no other method." Rather than cross swords with the old pastor, Albert instead became a very reticent student with the result that the pastor reported to Aunt Sophie that the boy was indifferent. "In reality," Albert later explained, "I was during those weeks so moved by the holiness of the time that I felt almost ill. When on Palm Sunday the whole company of us walked in procession from the vestry into the church, and Eugen Munch played 'Lift up your heads, O ye gates!' from Handel's *Messiah*, it was in wonderful harmony with the thoughts in my heart."

It was in Mulhouse, too, that Albert attended his first public concert. It was a splendid affair and the boy was outfitted in his Sunday best. The featured musician for the evening was a pianist of some renown by the name of Marie-Joseph Erb. Albert was overwhelmed by the superb ability of the pianist, and tried to imagine how Erb . . ."contrived to produce these cascades of arpeggios, these explosions of shooting stars, all the while retaining clarity in melody, achieving pianissimi in which no single notes were ever lost." Throughout the concert, Albert was full of excitement and wonder, having just enough understanding to recognize the greatness of the performance. "For me it was a startling revelation of all the possibilities of the piano." In the days to come, Albert labored over his lessons with new zeal and a dream of someday performing with the skill and talent of a Marie-Joseph Erb.

In 1893, the final examinations before graduation from the Gymnasium at Mulhouse took place. The oral part of the test was a very important occasion, and the boys were expected to wear formal clothes. Albert had to borrow trousers from his uncle, who was much shorter than the tall young man. There was nothing to do but wear them, and the whole class snickered when Albert walked into the room. The professor was very angry with Albert (above) for disturbing the class.

In the early summer of 1893, Albert began cramming for the final examinations before graduation from the Gymnasium at Mulhouse. The exams came in two phases. First there were the written tests, which Albert passed with little difficulty. Then came the oral test before the fearsome school commissioner, Professor Albrecht. All the students approached this confrontation with apprehension.

The oral test was an important occasion and, accordingly, it was the custom for the students to dress appropriately. For the boys, this consisted of starched collar, black tie, black trousers, and frock coat. Albert had a frock coat but no black trousers to complete the uniform. Uncle Louis promised the loan of his. A problem arose, however, because while Albert was now a tall, lean young man, Uncle Louis was short and stout. After trying on the trousers, Albert discovered that they barely reached to his high-topped shoes. To overcome this handicap, he added a length of string to his suspenders, which allowed the trousers to hang lower on his spare frame. When he donned the coat however, he saw with consternation that a gap existed between coat and trousers. Oh well! Too late to do anything about it now. And so, off to the examination room he went.

As Albert arrived in the room, some students began to snicker, causing others to turn around, and suddenly the whole room burst into gales of laughter at the sight of the distressed young man. Even the teachers from the school could not restrain themselves. But Professor

The professor who had been so angry with Albert for wearing such funny-looking clothes decided to quiz the young man himself. He concentrated on the subject of history, which fortunately was Albert's best subject. In a final address to the students after the exams were over, the professor complimented Albert on his fine showing (opposite).

Albrecht saw no humor in the situation and quickly restored the room to order. Glaring angrily at Schweitzer, the professor decided to quiz this young buffoon personally. Happily, the commissioner did not choose to test the boy on mathematics, and instead concentrated on the subject of history. In this, of course, Albert was at his very best, and soon the commissioner's irritation had melted away. In a final address to the students after the exams were over, Albrecht complimented Albert on his showing. On his graduation certificate, Albert found a note of praise from Commissioner Albrecht himself for his history examination.

And so, on June 18, 1893, Albert Schweitzer the boy became Albert Schweitzer the young man, as he passed another significant milestone on life's road. The formative years were over and the basic traits and characteristics that would make up Albert Schweitzer the man were already apparent.

It was an outwardly shy and reticent young man who left Mulhouse that summer. And yet there surged within him a complete faith and confidence in his future. The lessons in austerity and

discipline learned during his eight years with his aunt and uncle would serve him well in the years ahead. The devotion to duty, as exemplified by Dr. Wehmann, would mark all of Albert's future endeavors.

As Albert paused to look back over the preceding years, he felt a pang, almost of guilt, that he should have been granted such a happy youth. The question arose in his mind "whether this happiness was a thing that I might accept as a matter of course." As he toiled with these thoughts, "there grew up gradually within me an understanding of the saying of Jesus that we must not treat our lives as being for ourselves alone. Whoever is spared personal pain must feel himself called to help in diminishing the pain of others."

The means by which he would answer this call to help diminish pain had not yet taken form in the mind of the young man. For the present, he would embark upon his new studies in theology and philosophy at the University in Strasbourg. Twenty years would elapse before Doctor Schweitzer would meet his destiny on the banks of the Ogowe River in Africa.

Philosopher, Organist, Preacher

After the examinations at the Gymnasium were over, Albert returned to Günsbach for the summer. It was wonderful to be home again, amid the familiar surroundings of his youth and the warm love of his family. He no longer felt like a schoolboy and frequently emerged from his usual shell of reticence to involve himself in discussions of worldly subjects with his father and other learned men of the community.

Late in that summer of 1893, Albert received an invitation from his Uncle Charles to visit Paris. He had never before left his home province of Alsace and he was quick to accept the offer. He arrived in the French capital in early October, and set out to see the sights. He found that he was disappointed with Paris. He visited the Louvre and decided it could not compare with the museum at Colmar. In a letter home, he advised his parents that there really wasn't much of value in Paris.

Then one day his Aunt Mathilde suggested that Albert go to see the famous organ of St. Sulpice. This handsome organ had been built by the greatest organ builder in all Europe, Astride Cavaille-Col, some thirty years before. It was a monster instrument with five manuals and one hundred speaking stops. Albert was immediately enthused at the prospect of seeing and hearing this great organ. Aunt Mathilde

Late in the summer of 1893, Albert received an invitation from his Uncle Charles to visit Paris (opposite). During his visit, Albert went to see the famous organ of St. Sulpice, and met the great organist and composer, Charles Marie Widor. Albert played a Bach composition for Widor, who was so impressed with his playing that he offered to give him lessons. Widor helped Schweitzer become a master organ player.

gave him an introduction to Charles-Marie Widor, the great organist and composer, and Albert was off.

The streets were thronged that day with crowds celebrating the signing of a treaty between France and Russia. Thousands of Russian sailors milled about the streets and officers in full-dress white uniforms paraded along the boulevards. Colorful banners fluttered from lampposts. But none of this caught the eye of the visiting country boy from Alsace. As he pushed his way breathlessly through the crowds, he could think of only one thing—the great organ waiting at St. Sulpice.

Albert found Charles Widor seated before his organ. The introductions over, Widor, who wasted few words, said, "What will you play for me?" Without a moment's hesitation Schweitzer replied, "Why Bach of course." This was to be one of the truly memorable moments in Albert Schweitzer's life. He would play here many times in future days, but the memory of this first confrontation with the greatest organ in France would stay with him all the rest of his years.

As the first pure, powerful notes sounded through the nave of St. Sulpice, Albert was lost from all the world around him. In an oblivion of echoing tones, the young musician poured his soul into the cascade of sound that filled the church with a living beauty. Widor was visibly impressed by the profound depth of feeling and imagination that Albert expressed in his music. Rarely had he heard Bach played so profoundly. As the last trembling chord died away, Widor came to Albert and patted him on the back. "How would you like to come to me for lessons?" he asked. Though scarcely able to believe his ears, Albert managed to stammer a sincere "Yes." And so began a friendship which was to last for many years.

In later years, Schweitzer explained the influence Widor made on his music: "This instruction was for me an event of decisive importance. Widor led me on a fundamental improvement of my technique, and made me strive to attain perfect plasticity in playing. At the same time there dawned in me . . . the meaning of the architectonic in music."

Albert could stay in Paris only until the end of October, but now he had found something of value in the city. Charles Widor, the greatest French composer for the organ, was giving him, without charge, lessons on the greatest organ in France. The weeks sped by rapidly, and soon it was time for Albert to enter the University of Strasbourg. He sadly bid Widor good-bye and returned once more to Alsace.

Strasbourg is a lovely old medieval city on the river Ill in northern Alsace. With numerous bridges, narrow streets, and steep-roofed houses, a visitor to the city feels as if he is walking in a fairy tale. Above the whole scene towers the great cathedral spire. Albert Schweitzer loved Strasbourg from the very first. He would spend most of his next twenty years in this city.

Albert planned to major in theology, intending to become a pastor like his father. He also matriculated as a student of philosophy, but as a theology major he took up residence in the theological college of St. Thomas. There,

At the end of October, 1893, Albert left Paris to enter the University of Strasbourg, in a lovely old medieval city in northern Alsace. Opposite, a group of German students are shown celebrating the inauguration of the university under German direction in 1872. Schweitzer was to spend his next twenty years in Strasbourg, majoring in theology and philosophy, and then acting as pastor and teaching.

Albert Schweitzer (far left) is shown with his family when he was eighteen years old. From left to right, his father, Pastor Louis Schweitzer, his sisters Adele and Margerit, his sister Louise (seated), his mother, and his brother Paul.

in his quiet study overlooking the garden, he poured his vast energies into his heavy schedule.

One of Albert's first major hurdles was to pass the "Hebraicum," or preliminary examination in the Hebrew language. At the Gymnasium in Mulhouse he had not done well in Hebrew, and consequently his first term at Strasbourg was more difficult than it might have been. With much hard work, however, he successfully passed the examination in February of 1894. Not satisfied at barely getting by, Albert worked even harder at the strange language, which in time he came to master.

On April 1, 1894, now nineteen, he was called up for military service in the Prussian army. The one year of training was to be conducted in Alsace, and through the kindness of his captain, a man named Krull, Albert was allowed to continue his education and attendance at lectures whenever the regiment was near Strasbourg. On autumn maneuvers in Lower Alsace, Albert took along a copy of the Greek Testament to study in the evenings.

Schweitzer was somewhat of an enigma to his fellow soldiers. Scholars, they thought, were usually bespectacled sissies who would faint at the first hard work. But Albert was a tall, strong, raw-boned lad who could more than hold his own in pulling gun carriages out of the mud. He was a good soldier who obeyed orders quickly and without question. No goldbrick this quiet-spoken young man. And after a hard day of drilling and marching from early dawn to dusk, this son of a preacher from Günsbach would lie in his bedroll and study the gospels by candlelight. A rare soldier indeed. When his year of mili-

When Albert was nineteen years old, he was called up for military service in the Prussian army. Maneuvers (above) were conducted in Lower Alsace. After a hard day of drilling and marching from early dawn to dusk, Albert would lie in his bedroll and study the gospels by candlelight.

tary service was finished, Schweitzer returned to the university. He never expressed any resentment at this interruption in his studies.

Despite the tremendous burden of studying for degrees in both philosophy and theology, Albert still found time to pursue his musical career. He studied musical theory under Jacobsthal and, despite the man's bias against any music later than Beethoven's, Albert admitted that he got a thorough training.

He was delighted to find that Ernst Munch, brother of Eugen, was the organist at St. Wilhelm's Church at Strasbourg. Ernst immediately took up the teaching of young Albert where his brother had left off back in Mulhouse. Soon they were fast friends, and Schweitzer became virtually a member of the Munch family. Both soon were recognized leaders in the Bach cult that sprang up in Strasbourg in the 1890's.

"It meant a considerable help to my musical studies that Ernst Munch entrusted to me the organ accompaniment of the Cantatas and the Passion music at the Bach concerts given by the choir of St. Wilhelm's," Albert wrote later. But Schweitzer could not be satisfied with studying Bach alone. "Together with my veneration for Bach went the same feeling for Richard Wagner." In 1896, Albert was given tickets to the second complete performance of Wagner's Tetralogy at Bayreuth. The first had taken place twenty years before, when Albert was only one year old. Albert scrimped and saved his money and finally had enough to make the trip by limiting himself to only one meal per day. The performance made a lasting impression on him and he later

would write that Wagner's works were "unique; a miracle of creative power."

On his way home from Bayreuth, he stopped in Stuttgart to see the new organ at the Liederhalle. The instrument was already famous throughout Europe and Schweitzer had to hear it for himself. He was very much disillusioned by the experience. This handsome and very expensive new instrument could not compare in tone and clarity to the old organs he had played. "Why?" he asked himself. He finally decided that the art of organ building was a fading art. With this belief in mind, a seed was born which, in the years to come, would bear fruit as a book about the construction of organs.

Late in the summer of 1897, Albert, along with the other theology students, received the subject for his thesis. His grades on this thesis would determine whether he would be allowed to take the first theological examination. The subject as given was, "Schleiermacher's teaching about the Last Supper compared with the conceptions of it embodied in the New Testament and the confessions of faith drawn up by the Reformers." Only eight weeks were given for completion, and Albert threw himself into the task with renewed energy. With the thesis finished to the satisfaction of the faculty, Schweitzer continued his studies for the examination. On May 6, 1898, he passed the examination for a doctorate in theology and now turned his energies to the study of philosophy.

Schweitzer studied philosophy under Theobald Ziegler who suggested that he take as a subject the religious philosophy of Kant. Albert had received the Goll scholarship, which amounted to

1200 marks ($240) per year. With this small stipend, he decided to go to Paris and study at the Sorbonne. There he would also be able to study the organ once again under his friend Widor.

Disappointed in the methods of instruction at the Sorbonne, Albert neglected his studies but, nevertheless, worked diligently on his thesis. It was during this long cold winter of 1898-99 that Widor convinced Albert that he should write a book relating Bach's symbolism to the old Lutheran cantatas and masses. Once again, Schweitzer took upon himself a task that he would be many years in completing. The book, finally published in 1905, had been written in French at the request of Widor.

In the spring of 1899, Albert returned once more to his beloved Günsbach where he put the final touches on his study of Kant. He then journeyed off to Berlin. In the German capital, Schweitzer attended lectures on philosophy and also attended organ recitals. He was disappointed in both the Berlin organists and organs.

Schweitzer was, however, impressed with the city of Berlin and its spirit and intellectual life. The Berlin of the turn of the century was a charming, almost provincial city. This was more than fourteen years before the goose-stepping armies of the Kaiser tramped the city's streets. More than three decades would pass before the Nazi *swastika* fluttered from the rooftops and cries of *Sieg Heil* echoed from the *Reichstag*. Later, Schweitzer would write, "Thus I came to know Berlin at the finest period of its existence, and to love it."

In July of 1899, Albert returned to Strasbourg and spent the next year cramming for examinations. First came his examination in philosophy, and he was awarded a doctorate soon after his return from Berlin. His dissertation on the religious philosophy of Kant was published as a book later that year. Now he could devote all his studies toward getting his theological licentiate. The licentiate is a grade higher than the doctorate he already had and would qualify him as a full professor. In the meantime, he commenced serving the required term as a deacon, prior to his second exam in theology. At last, on July 15, 1900, Albert Schweitzer took his examination and received his degree of licentiate in theology *"magna cum laude."*

On September 23, 1900, Albert was ordained a regular curate at St. Nicholas Church in Strasbourg. For his small pay of 100 marks, about $20, per month, Albert was required to preach afternoon sermons, the Sunday children's service, and teach the confirmation classes. Occasionally he would have a free Sunday, when he would ride the train to Günsbach. There he would take the service for his father at the little church he knew and loved so well. "To me preaching was a necessity of my being," he would write later. "I felt it as something wonderful that I was allowed to address a congregation every Sunday about the deepest question of life."

And so, as the new century dawned full of promise, Albert Schweitzer was finished with his formal studies. He was twenty-five years old, a learned man in music, theology, and philosophy. Five years remained to live his life for himself. Five years in which to reach for fame and intellectual satisfaction. At the end of that time he must make a decision: find the answer to the most burning question in his heart—"How to serve humanity?" The promise he had made when he was twenty-one would not be forgotten. Five years remained to find the key to his destiny.

In 1899, Albert went to Berlin (opposite) to attend lectures on philosophy and to hear organ recitals. He was disappointed in both the Berlin organists and organs, but he was impressed with the city itself and its spirit and intellectual life. It was a charming city, and Albert grew to love it.

End of the Search

With his studies and examinations out of the way, Albert Schweitzer could now pour his heart and energies into his music and his writings. As a curate, he could now look forward to three months per year of vacation. One month came in the spring. During this period he liked to visit Paris and continue his organ studies with Widor. He spent his autumn holiday writing in his beloved hometown of Günsbach.

His writings at this time were devoted mainly to his study of Bach and his book on organ building. But soon he began his great work entitled, "The Quest for the Historical Jesus," which would take him four years to complete.

In 1901, Schweitzer was appointed provisional principal for the Theological College and administrative responsibility was added to his burdens. But Schweitzer was always happiest when his energies were taxed to the fullest. He still found time to pursue his social work as a member of a student association known as the Diaconate of St. Thomas. This group was concerned with helping the poor families of Strasbourg. After taking up collections, they pedaled about on their bicycles interviewing the sick and poor, finding the true needs of the people and bringing aid.

As for Albert, he was still searching for the means by which he could keep his promise to himself. How would he finally decide to devote his life to serving humanity? Perhaps among the poor and destitute children of Alsace. Perhaps with vagrants and discharged prisoners. The years were flying by and still he had not found the answer. The search would continue.

One of the students who worked with the Diaconate of St. Thomas was a girl by the name of Helene Bresslau. She was a pretty, dark-haired Jewish girl whose father was a famous Strasbourg historian. Albert was drawn to this energetic young lady and she was impressed by him. Unknown to Albert, Helene Bresslau had also made a promise to herself. She planned to live for herself to the age of twenty-five, at which time she would offer her life to the service of mankind. She, too, was in search of her destiny which, although neither could suspect it in 1901, would be forever intertwined with that of Albert Schweitzer.

The months rolled by and in 1903, Albert was named permanent principal of the college. He now moved to the spacious official quarters overlooking the embankment of St. Thomas. The

In 1901, Schweitzer was appointed provisional principal for the theological college at Strasbourg. He still found time, however, to pursue other interests, among which was his social work among the poor families of the city. He spent much time pedaling about on his bicycle interviewing the sick and poor (left) to find their true needs and to bring them aid.

young principal was an immediate hit with the students. He was well known, even famous, for his learning, and this, of course, earned the respect of the student body. It was his youth, however, that most impressed the students. He was young enough to be able to share their point of view and to join in their jokes. They looked with great pride upon a person, not so much older than they, who had earned the respect and acceptance of the university fathers.

These were happy, wonderful years for Albert Schweitzer. He had an honored position with the university, he was beginning to reap rewards from his books in the form of royalties, and he had a considerable amount of leisure time to devote to the things he loved best—his preaching, his music, and his writing. He traveled quite a lot, especially in search of material for his book about organs. He also accompanied his Aunt Mathilde to Öberammergau for the Passion Play. In his travels he came in contact with great people and great minds. At Bayreuth he met Cosima Wagner, daughter of Liszt. In Paris he met the Countess de Pourteles and Princess Metternich. On another visit to Paris he met Romain Rolland, the playwright, poet, historian, and biographer.

Rolland was an idealist, too, greatly concerned with the idea of a united Europe which transcended national fears and interests. For all his interest in international and political affairs, Rolland was something of a recluse. He lived and labored in a small attic overlooking the Boulevard Montparnasse. Here Albert Schweitzer spent many hours discussing with Rolland the dreams and ethics they both treasured —a spiritual unity among men.

Through his exchange of thought with Rolland, Schweitzer broadened his international horizon to some extent. The two discussed such current international issues as the Russo–Japanese War and President Theodore Roosevelt's successful efforts as mediator. They also discussed the growing tension between France and Germany over their conflicting interests in Morocco.

The work that most absorbed Schweitzer during this period was his "Quest for the Historical Jesus." In researching this work he studied every account of Jesus' life that had been written during the last three centuries. His study was filled with stacks of books, each representing a chapter in his forthcoming work. Visitors, he reported later, "had to thread their way across the room along paths which ran between heaps of books." His cleaning lady had to be constantly warned to "Leave those books alone!"

One might have expected Albert Schweitzer to settle for life in the quiet routine at St. Thomas. No one knew, however, that he was searching desperately for a meaningful way to devote his life to humanity. "What I wanted," he recalled later, "was an absolutely personal and independent activity. Although I was resolved to put my service at the disposal of some organization, if it should be really necessary, I nevertheless never gave up the hope of finding a sphere of activity to which I could devote myself as an individual and as wholly free."

Then, in the fall of 1904, he found the answer in the magazine of the Paris Missionary Society. For awhile he con-

---

These years at the university were happy ones for Albert Schweitzer. He had an honored position there and also had a considerable amount of time to devote to the things he loved best—his preaching, his music, and his writing. He traveled a lot and once accompanied his Aunt Mathilde to Öberammergau for the Passion Play (opposite).

During his years at Strasbourg,
Schweitzer was searching
desperately for a meaningful
way to devote his life to
humanity. This photograph was
taken when he was thirty years
old, the year he decided to study
medicine, become a doctor, and
go to Africa to fulfill what he
had determined to be his mission
in life.

*"...what I wanted was an absolutely
personal and independent activity..."*

fided his plan to no one as he pondered the ultimate question of how to serve. A few months later came his thirtieth birthday and with it the decision to become a doctor. By now, he and Helene had agreed to marry, and to her he confessed his plan to study medicine and go to Africa. She gave her whole-hearted support.

The decision made, Schweitzer began to ponder like the man in the parable who "desiring to build a tower, first counts the cost whether he have here-with to complete it." His sacrifice would be great. He would sever his ties, per-haps forever, with his beloved Vosges Mountains and Günsbach. He must leave behind the beautiful organs and the music which had been so much a part of his life. The peaceful life of a respected college principal would be lost forever. The cost would indeed be high.

Schweitzer decided to make one small concession to his existing way of life. He would give himself one more year to complete his book on Bach and his

"Quest for the Historical Jesus." He set to work with a frenzy.

On Friday, the thirteenth of October, 1905, Schweitzer dropped a packet of letters in a mail box in Paris. One was to his parents in Günsbach, others to his closest friends. In the letters he explained his decision that "at the be-ginning of the winter term I should enter myself as a medical student, in order to go later on to Equatorial Africa as a doctor." In another letter he sent his resignation as principal of St. Thomas Theological College. The news came as a rather severe shock to everyone.

Immediately, Schweitzer remembered later, "I had hard battles to fight with relations and friends." Widor scolded him for "being like a general who wanted to go into the firing line with a rifle." Some were indignant that he had not confided in them of his plans. Romain Rolland was noncommittal.

Despite all persuasion, Schweitzer could not be swayed. "I held the venture to be justified," he wrote later, "because

I had considered it for a long time and from every point of view, and credited myself with the possession of health, sound nerves, energy, practical common sense, toughness, prudence, very few wants, and everything else that might be found necessary by anyone wandering along the path of the idea." He did not discount the possibility of failure, however. But he believed himself to have "the protective armor of a temperament quite capable of enduring an eventual failure of my plan."

Schweitzer the medical student now moved to four small rooms in the attic across the courtyard from his spacious former offices. These cluttered little rooms were to be his home for the next seven years. Late in October of 1905 he attended his first lectures in anatomy.

The years ahead were ones of immense strain and fatigue, even for the seemingly tireless Schweitzer. He continued giving lectures in theology and preached nearly every Sunday. Now that he no longer received his stipend

as principal of the college, he had to find other means of support. As he was now considered one of the great organists of Europe, he was invited to play in many recitals and concerts. He made frequent trips to Paris and one to Barcelona where his fees provided a new source of income.

The science of medicine proved to be the most difficult subject Schweitzer had ever studied. From long years of thinking in abstract terms, he was turned suddenly to a world of realities and exact details. When exam time came around he was coaxed into joining a "cramming club" with his younger fellow students. By studying questions asked in previous years the students were able to guess in advance what questions would be on the forthcoming exams. Schweitzer passed the exams more easily than he had expected.

His final state medical examinations in 1911 extended from October to December. The strain was terrific on Schweitzer, who was now nearing thirty-seven years of age. But all the tests were successfully passed and the terrible ordeal was over at last. Ahead lay one year of internship and work on his doctoral thesis—then Africa.

He immediately began preparing for the journey to the Dark Continent. He took a course in tropical medicine in Paris and contacted the Paris Missionary Society. Some of his theological writings had differed somewhat with the views of the society, and it was only after Schweitzer had promised to remain "silent as a fish" that they accepted him solely as a doctor of medicine.

On June 18, 1912, Albert and Helene were married in Strasbourg. With his new bride, Schweitzer moved to his father's parsonage in Günsbach for the final months of preparation. There, with Helene's assistance, he compiled the long lists of drugs and medical supplies he estimated he would need for a two-

year stay in Africa. Since about $10,000 would be needed for the purchase of these supplies, Schweitzer began giving concerts to raise the funds. He also found it necessary to ask donations of friends and associates. By the end of 1912 the money had been raised.

At last he was ready. In February of 1913, he sent some seventy packing cases of supplies to Bordeaux by train. A last round of good-byes to friends in Strasbourg was followed by a journey home to Günsbach. There, on Good Friday, he kissed his parents good-bye and waved farewell to his native village as the train left for Paris.

On Easter Sunday he played the organ at St. Sulpice for the last time. When he finished, the Paris Bach Society presented him with a lead-lined piano in appreciation of long years of service as their organist. That afternoon the Schweitzers left for Bordeaux where the S.S. *Europe* waited to carry them to Africa.

Schweitzer's final medical examinations were passed in December, 1911, when he was thirty-seven years old. He spent another year as an intern while he made preparations to practice medicine for the Paris Missionary Society. He married Helene Bresslau in June of 1912, and at last, in April, 1913, some seventy packing cases of supplies were loaded aboard the S.S. Europe (above) for the long journey with Dr. and Mrs. Schweitzer to Lambaréné, Africa.

And so, as war clouds darkened the horizons of Europe, Albert Schweitzer sailed away in search of a way to best serve his fellowman. Europe watched him go with wagging heads and shrugging shoulders. Few could comprehend his motives. Not many months would pass before Europe was engulfed in flames as the most inhumane war yet known to man burned its way across the map. The minds and hearts of men were turned once more to slaughter and destruction.

But in the steaming jungle along the Ogowe River, Albert Schweitzer was waging his own war against disease and pain. The militarists of Europe would never understand his motives. From Lambaréné, the jungle doctor would explain:

"That everyone shall exert himself to practice true humanity toward his fellowmen, on that depends the future of mankind!"

Reverence for Life

On his first day at Lambaréné, Dr. Schweitzer inspected his new surroundings. The sight was enough to send a less-determined soul scurrying back to Europe. The Paris Missionary Society had promised him a hospital. True, it was not supposed to have been anything substantial, and Schweitzer was prepared to make do with whatever was available. As it turned out, there was no hospital waiting for him at Lambaréné.

Undeterred, Dr. Schweitzer looked around for any available building. The only thing unoccupied was a nearby chicken coop. It was in a sad state of repair and featured an earthen floor and cracking walls, both covered with filth, and no roof. The doctor shrugged his shoulders, rolled up his sleeves, and set to work. The floor was soon scraped and cleaned, the walls scrubbed and whitewashed, and shelves installed. A palm-leaf roof soon kept out most of the rain or blazing sunshine. An old camp bed served as an operating table. Dr. Schweitzer was in business.

The variety of the diseases and illnesses shocked Schweitzer at first. From miles around, natives came with such illnesses as malaria, dysentery, ulcers, hernias, and the dreaded sleeping sickness spread by the tsetse flies. And, of course, there were the most pathetic of all—the lepers.

It was obvious right from the start that larger quarters were needed. Many of the patients needed constant care if they were to recover. Dr. Schweitzer now attacked a new challenge and a new line of work—that of construction engineer and foreman. He recruited the members of families who invariably accompanied the patients and organized them into work crews. Pleading, threatening, bribing, and cajoling, he managed to oversee the construction of a new hospital down by the river.

The new building was fairly small, only twenty-six feet long by thirteen feet wide, but it was more substantial than the chicken house. Made of corrugated iron walls, a concrete floor, and

---

Dr. Schweitzer discovered immediately that the hospital the Paris Missionary Society had promised him did not exist in Lambaréné. Undeterred, Schweitzer looked around for an available building to use as a hospital. The only thing unoccupied was a chicken coop—very dirty and in a sad state of disrepair. The doctor set to work (opposite) to make the building usable, and soon the floor was scraped and cleaned, the walls were scrubbed and whitewashed, and shelves were installed. A palm-leaf roof was put up and an old camp bed was brought in to serve as an operating table.

palm-leaf roof, it contained a small consulting room, a dispensary, and an operating room. He moved to this building in the fall of 1913 and by the end of the year some outer buildings of bamboo had been constructed to house the patients.

Mme. Schweitzer was the doctor's chief helper during these early months. She had a capacity for hard work that nearly matched the doctor's. She cleaned the surgical instruments, tended the very sick with special care, administered anesthetics on operating days, and superintended the linens and bandages. Of her help, Dr. Schweitzer later wrote, "That she managed successfully the complicated work of an African household, and yet could find every day some hours to spare for the hospital was really a wonderful achievement."

Dr. Schweitzer soon found another assistant of real value. Joseph Azoawami was a man who had come to the doctor as a patient and stayed on as Schweitzer's right-hand man. Joseph could speak French and knew many of the African dialects. Although he could not read or write, Joseph quickly learned the shapes of the letters on medicine bottles and was soon administering to patients on directions from the doctor.

Joseph was a valuable link between the doctor and his patients and offered much sound advice. He felt quite strongly, however, that the doctor should not accept as patients those people who were obviously beyond help. This was the way the native fetish doctors preserved their reputations in the jungles.

But Dr. Schweitzer could never adopt such a philosophy. Instead, he adopted the policy of being brutally frank with his patients. "To native patients one must tell the truth without reservation," he wrote later. "They wish to know it and they can endure it, for death is to them something natural. They are not afraid of it, but face it calmly. If, after all, the patient unexpectedly recovers, so much the better for the doctor's reputation. He ranks thereafter as one who can cure even fatal diseases."

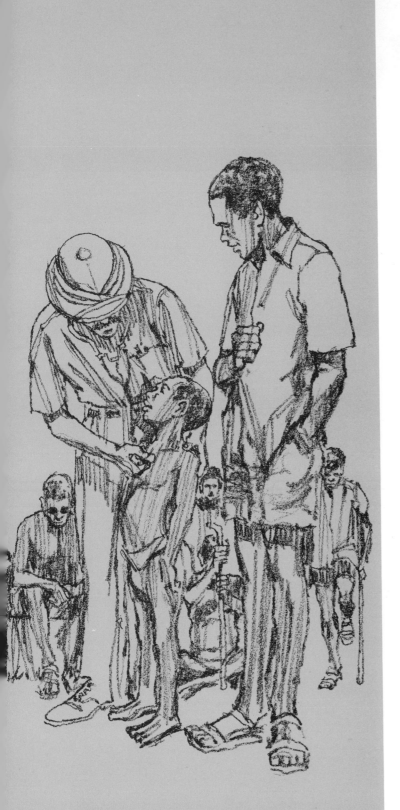

Above: Dr. Schweitzer and his assistant, Joseph Azoawami, treating patients. Joseph was a former patient who stayed on to help the doctor. He knew French and many African dialects and proved to be invaluable as an interpreter and Dr. Schweitzer's right-hand man.

The strain of life, and a doctor's practice, in the jungle at times became almost unbearable. At night came the malaria-carrying mosquitoes. During the day the tsetse flies spread their infectious disease. In the winter, equatorial rains drenched the region and in the summer a dry, blazing heat baked the land. Occasionally, the little mission would become an armed camp under the generalship of Dr. Schweitzer as everyone turned out to do battle with an army of traveler ants. These terrifying little creatures march in columns of five or six abreast and lay waste to everything in their path. They are unafraid of man or beast, and only fire or chemicals can turn them back.

Other dangers lurked nearby. Windows had to be barred against marauding leopards. Some poisonous snakes and boa constrictors inhabited the undergrowth. Crocodiles lived in nearby swamps and along the banks of the river. The night, the day, the water, the land, the jungle, the clearings—all, in the natural way of things, hid a potential danger to health or to life itself.

To relieve the tension, Dr. Schweitzer turned once more to his music. In those past days of strain when he was studying medicine, he had been able to refresh himself by playing the organ with his friend Ernst Munch. Now, in the hot evenings on the Ogowe, he turned to his lead-lined piano. As the music of Bach, Mendelssohn, and Widor echoed from the little house to fill the jungle night with a new sound, the tensions and pressures of the day drained slowly from the tired shoulders of Albert Schweitzer.

The months passed by swiftly, and in this place where time stood still, the doctor took little note of the world he had left behind. In Europe, war clouds were gathering rapidly and armies were on the march. Across the sea, President Wilson was resorting to force of arms at Veracruz and the United States and Mexico were close to war. The Mexico–United States dispute was successfully mediated at the ABC Conference in

59

"...there suddenly flashed
upon my mind, unforeseen
and unsought, the phrase,
'Reverence for Life.'"

Canada in June of 1914. But in Europe peace efforts failed. On August 3, Schweitzer's native country, Germany, declared war on France.

Two days later, on August 5, 1914, a party of French colonial soldiers came to the Schweitzer house at Lambaréné and placed the doctor and his wife under house arrest. Schweitzer was dismayed, but helpless. The medical work at Lambaréné came to an end. For four months, Schweitzer tried to fill his hours by writing a book about the decay and restoration of civilization. Meanwhile, his friends in Paris—Widor and the Paris Bach Society especially—were using their influence to effect his release. Late in November an order came from the Resident-General of Gabon giving him permission to continue his work. The little hospital opened its doors once more.

Now new problems threatened. With the war on, drugs and medical supplies would be hard to come by. Even food, except that which could be procured locally, would be difficult to find. The coming months would require the utmost patience and resourcefulness.

The war and all its horrible manifestations haunted the sensitive mind of Albert Schweitzer. What was to become of civilization? Why must men murder and destroy? Something must be lacking in the spirit of man. Civilization with all its wonders of invention and material progress had not discovered or acknowledged a link with the basic goodness of Christianity. There was a mutual relationship between the spiritual and the material, he decided, but how can it be expressed?

For weeks Dr. Schweitzer pondered his problem as he sought to find the key words or phrase to express what he felt in his heart. Then one night in September, 1915, as he rode a steamer up the river to tend a sick missionary, there suddenly "flashed upon my mind, unforseen and unsought, the phrase, 'Reverence for Life.'"

The phrase, as he has written of it, expresses more than simply one's own will to live. Its acceptance recognizes the will to live in all forms of life. It acknowledges not only the will to live, but the right to live of others. It expresses more than the relationship of man to man, but also "his attitude to the world and all life that comes within his reach."

In German the phrase is *Erfurcht vor dem Leben* and upon these four words Albert Schweitzer laid the foundation of his philosophy. Henceforth, for all the days of his life, he would devote himself to the preservation of life in all living things. He recognized that at times it was necessary to kill one form of life to permit others to survive. For such a crime he would stand in judgment. But no life must be needlessly taken. No grasses needlessly trammeled, no insects wantonly crushed. Man, who alone has the capacity to think, must celebrate life as the supreme wonder.

Schweitzer had come from Europe to bring light to the Dark Continent. Now Europe itself was in darkness. But in a jungle clearing on the banks of the Ogowe River, a light flickered in the heart and mind of a missionary doctor. "Sooner or later," he wrote, "there must dawn the true and final Renaissance which will bring peace to the world." It must begin, he knew, with a reverence for life.

The months passed and, despite a shortage of drugs and medicines, Dr. Schweitzer continued his work. In September of 1917, an order came from the Clemenceau government in Paris for all enemy aliens in the French Empire to be rounded up and shipped to France for internment. Native soldiers came at once to the doctor's house in Lambaréné

In September of 1917, after France had taken over
Dr. Schweitzer's native Alsace during World War I,
an order came from the government in Paris for all
enemy aliens in the French Empire to be rounded up
and shipped to France for internment. Dr. Schweitzer
and his wife were taken back to France and prison.
The hospital ceased to exist. At the prison in Garaison
(opposite), Schweitzer (above) found an opportunity
to learn. He looked upon the camp and its inmates
as a sort of international university that required no
books. He learned much, but he also gave much, for
he became the camp doctor and brought his medical
knowledge and aid to the sick.

and in a few hours the hospital ceased
to exist. The great work of the past
four and a half years was over. Tired
and weary from the strain of life in the
jungle, Dr. and Mme. Schweitzer slowly
packed their few belongings, stored the
medical supplies in a corrugated iron
shed, and boarded the *Afrique* for the
journey back to France and prison.

The voyage was filled with boredom.
The Schweitzers were under constant guard and were forbidden to have
any visitors. For a couple of hours each
day they were allowed on deck, but
otherwise were confined to their cabin.
At last the ship arrived in Bordeaux,
the port from which they had sailed so
bravely more than four years before.
After three weeks in a barracks called
the Caserne de Passage, they were transferred to Garaison in the Pyrenees
Mountains. Here the Schweitzers would
remain for the next several months.

The prison in Garaison was an old
monastery with a high enclosed courtyard and long rambling corridors. Both
Dr. and Mme. Schweitzer had been
ill, but now, in the cold, crisp air blow-
ing down from the Pyrenees, Mme.
Schweitzer's health began to improve.
The doctor still suffered from dysentery,
but with the drugs he still possessed he
began to tend to himself. Their fellow
inmates came from all walks of life and
from many nations of the world. Many,
such as artists, tailors, shoemakers,
hotel managers, and waiters, had been
caught in Paris when the war began.
Many others, like the Schweitzers, had
been caught in the colonies. There were
Germans, Austrians, Turks, Arabs,
Greeks, and Orientals.

As usual, Albert Schweitzer found in
his predicament an opportunity to
learn. He looked upon the camp and its
inmates as a sort of international university that required no books. In numerous discussions, "about banking,
architecture, factory building and
equipment, cereal growing, furnace
building, and many other things, I
picked up information which I should
probably never have acquired else-

where." He, in turn, became the camp doctor and brought his medical knowledge and aid to the sick.

In March of 1918, the Schweitzers were transferred to another camp, this one at St. Rémy. Here they met other Alsatians including a Günsbach schoolmaster and a young pastor who had been one of Schweitzer's students at Strasbourg. Then, in July, they were taken to Switzerland where they were to be exchanged for prisoners being held in Germany. In Zurich, friends who had heard of his coming greeted him at the station. After a brief stop, the train pushed on to Constance, Germany, where the terrible toll of war was clearly evident. Everyone seemed in despair and misery.

Mme. Schweitzer was immediately allowed to go to Strasbourg and her parent's home, while the doctor remained in Constance to complete the necessary formalities. Then he, too, left for Strasbourg, which was blacked out against possible air attack. Because Günsbach was very near the fighting front, it was days before Schweitzer could receive the required permit to return home. The train ran only as far as Colmar and from there Schweitzer had to walk. As he trod the little road he had known so well as a boy, his heart grew heavy at the sight. The beautiful forests on the hillsides were gone; only scorched stumps remained. Quiet farmhouses he remembered from youth lay in crumbled piles of masonry and stone. Barbed wire fenced the road, and at every turning there was a brick machine-gun emplacement. He was almost afraid to make the last turn which would bring Günsbach into view. What would be left?

And then at last, there was Günsbach, hidden deep among the hills, safe from the artillery shells. His heart filled with joy and thanksgiving as he quickened his pace down the winding road to his father's home. His father was safe and sound and had grown accustomed to the sounds of battle nearby. He had even become indifferent to the dangers of bombardment and refused to take

shelter in the cellar. But Albert's mother was no longer there. In one of those terrible accidents of war she had been trampled to death by cavalry on the road to Weierim-Tal in 1916.

It soon developed that Schweitzer needed an operation, and in late August he returned to Strasbourg for treatment. As soon as his health permitted, Schweitzer accepted a position as a doctor in the municipal hospital and about the same time was appointed curate at St. Nicolas' once again. With his wife, he then moved into a parsonage on the embankment.

In November of 1918, World War I at last came to an end, and Alsace came once more under French rule. Across the Rhine, people were starving as the German nation crumbled in chaos. But in Strasbourg, Dr. Albert Schweitzer eked out a modest living and quietly nursed his health. The worst was past and once again his thoughts turned to Lambaréné in the African jungle. Perhaps in the aftermath of the most terrible war in history, the civilizations of Europe would see the light and grasp in their hearts the meaning of reverence for life. Dr. Schweitzer would gather new strength and resources in the months ahead. From an enlightened Europe he would someday return with new hope and new promise to the little mission station on the banks of the Ogowe River.

In 1918, the Schweitzers were exchanged for prisoners being held in Germany. When Schweitzer finally arrived at Colmar, he walked through the war-torn countryside (below) toward Günsbach. His heart was heavy as he saw the ruins, but Günsbach, hidden deep among the hills, had been spared. His father was safe, though his mother had been killed during the war. Schweitzer returned to Strasbourg as curate of St. Nicholas' and with his wife moved into the parsonage there.

65

The Years of Fame

On Dr. Schweitzer's forty-fourth birthday, January 14, 1919, Mme. Schweitzer presented him her most unique birthday gift—a baby girl. The doctor named his daughter Rhena in honor of the river Rhine. Thus, the new year dawned full of hope and promise. There was peace in the world and Dr. Schweitzer's health was gradually improving here in the shadow of his beloved Vosges Mountains.

The months passed swiftly and, following a second operation, Dr. Schweitzer's good health returned. Hale and hearty once more, his thoughts turned again to Lambaréné. A few days before Christmas, 1919, he received an invitation to deliver a series of lectures at the University of Uppsala in Sweden. As the guest of the Archbishop Soderman, Dr. Schweitzer found renewed

vigor in the stimulating climate of Sweden. His final lecture was devoted to the concept of reverence for life. His audience was enthusiastic and, he would write later, "I found for the first time an echo to the thoughts I had been carrying about with me for five years." The tremendous reception to his philosophy of *Erfurcht vor dem Leben* left him speechless and he stood with his head bowed in silence as the cheers swept up to him from the auditorium.

He now decided that he must return to Lambaréné and continue the work which had been interrupted in 1917. But it would take much money to get started again. He wondered how to raise it. Archbishop Soderman had the answer. "Give lectures about your jungle hospital," he advised, "and play organ recitals. You will see, people will

In 1919, Dr. Schweitzer was invited to deliver a series of lectures at the University of
Uppsala in Sweden. His philosophy of "Reverence for Life" was received with enthusi-
asm by his Swedish audiences (left).
Schweitzer decided at this time that he must
return to Lambaréné to continue the work
that had been interrupted in 1917, and it was
suggested that he give lectures and organ recitals to raise the necessary funds. By February, 1924, he was ready, and sailed for
Africa with a young English student as his
assistant. His wife, Helene, was ill and un-
able to accompany him.

---

pay to hear you and in no time you will
have all the money you need to return
to Lambaréné."

Schweitzer took the Archbishop at
his word, and for the next two years he
delivered lectures and gave organ recitals all over Europe. He also continued
his writing and in 1921 a book about his
life and work in Africa was published,
entitled *Zwischen Wasser und Urwald*
("On the Edge of the Primeval Forest").
In 1923 his first two volumes of *The
Philosophy of Civilization* were printed.
By the end of 1923 he was ready. Mme.
Schweitzer was ill again and could not
accompany him, but a young English
college student, Noel Gillespie, came
along as his assistant. On February 21,
1924, they sailed for Africa.

On the nineteenth of April, Easter
Eve, he arrived once more in Lamba-

réné. Only the walls of the hospital remained. The roof and outer buildings had all decayed and collapsed. The jungle had reclaimed much of the little clearing he had left seven years before.

The doctor and Noel set to work, and after many months of labor, the hospital was returned to its previous state. During that period, Schweitzer was a doctor in the morning and a carpenter in the afternoon. It was tiring work, but by the fall of 1925 the building and clearing were complete.

Conditions improved perceptibly during 1925. Two doctors and two nurses arrived from Europe to become members of Schweitzer's hospital staff. A surprise gift from his friends in Sweden arrived one day which pleased the doctor immensely. It was a twenty-eight-foot motorboat especially designed for river navigation in shallow water. The boat was named *Tak sa mycket*, which in Swedish means, "Many Thanks."

It soon became clear that a new hospital was needed. The present one was filled to overflowing. There was no room for expansion at the present site, so one day Dr. Schweitzer took his boat in search of a new place to build a hospital.

He found just the spot some two miles upstream from the original station. The district commissioner immediately granted the doctor's request for nearly 200 acres of land and the long hard job of construction began.

Weeks of exhausting labor turned into months, and the months into a year, when finally, in January of 1927, the new hospital was ready for occupancy. It was a splendid improvement over the old. There was now room for 200 patients and excellent quarters for the hospital staff. There were isolation wards for dysentery patients, and other buildings set apart for the mentally ill. There were wooden floors in the new huts and double-deck bunks which offered more comfort to the patients. "So now," Dr. Schweitzer would write, "for the first time since I began to work in Africa my patients were housed as human beings should be!"

On July 21, 1927, Dr. Schweitzer left Lambaréné and returned to Europe and his family, whom he had not seen in three and a half years. Tired and ailing again, he looked forward to peace and quiet. He purchased a little house near Königsfeld in the Black Forest and be-

---

When he arrived in Lambaréné, Dr. Schweitzer found that only the walls of the hospital remained. The jungle had reclaimed much of the clearing he had left seven years before. The doctor and his assistant, Noel Gillespie, set to work and repaired the hospital. In 1925, Schweitzer's staff increased with the arrival of two doctors and two nurses from Europe. Also in that year, it became clear that the present hospital was far too small. A new site was found and after a year of exhausting labor (opposite), a new hospital was ready for occupancy.

gan to devote his time to his writing.

But fame was beginning to catch up with Albert Schweitzer, the Doctor of Lambaréné. There was a constant stream of requests from all over Europe to give organ recitals or lectures on theology or his activities in Africa. In August of 1928, he was awarded the Goethe Prize for "services to humanity." At Günsbach he built a new house on the road to Münster to be used as a haven of rest for doctors and nurses returning from service at Lambaréné.

During the twelve years from 1927 to 1939, Dr. Schweitzer made the trip to and from Lambaréné many times. While in Europe he gave his lectures and recitals and also made records of his organ playing. Back in Lambaréné he contin-

ued the task of adding and improving the facilities of the hospital. The mission now boasted a thriving orchard, new wards, and a small plantation.

During this period his fame continued to grow. Britain honored him with honorary degrees from Oxford, St. Andrews, and Edinburgh. Wherever he went he was feted and acclaimed. In early 1937 he sailed to Africa for the sixth time, worried again about the war clouds that were gathering over Europe.

After a two-year absence, he returned in February of 1939 to France. There he heard the threats and ravings of Adolf Hitler. Albert Schweitzer, this gentle man who believed that all life is sacred, was appalled by the bloodlust sweeping over Germany. Now he knew

that Europe was doomed. Not even bothering to unpack his baggage, Schweitzer hurried to Günsbach and moved his wife and daughter to Switzerland. Then, alone, he boarded a ship for the return to Africa after a stay in Europe of less than two weeks.

The fall of France in 1940 and the subsequent forming of a puppet government friendly to the Germans, at Vichy, resulted in a civil war in Gabon. The Governor of Gabon gave his allegiance to the Vichy regime but many colonists in the area cast their lot with the Free French under General De Gaulle. Soon fighting spread to the very gates of Lambaréné and Dr. Schweitzer was concerned for his patients and staff. Both sides, however, respected the hospital and only a few stray shots fell within the hospital compound. The Free French, on the side of the Allies, won control of the region and peace came again to Lambaréné.

Dr. Schweitzer went back to Europe to see his family in 1927, and stayed there to write and lecture, rest and give organ recitals, for the next twelve years. During this time, he made several trips back to Lambaréné. By 1937, war again seemed to be threatening in Europe, and by 1939, Schweitzer decided to move his family to Switzerland and safety. He himself returned to Africa. War came very close to Lambaréné (below), but the hospital compound was not harmed and peace eventually returned to the region.

71 *(text continued on page 86)*

Far left: Dr. Schweitzer in his study during his early years at Lambaréné. Left: He is shown in July, 1949, at the age of seventy-four, when he received an honorary law degree from the University of Chicago.

Left: Dr. Schweitzer as he appeared in 1952 when he received the Nobel Peace Prize. Opposite, top, he delivers his Nobel Prize lecture to an Oslo, Norway, audience in 1954. Opposite, bottom, the doctor and his wife are greeted by their friends in Günsbach during a 1956 visit.

Opposite, Dr. Schweitzer en route to his hospital in French Equatorial Africa shortly after his eightieth birthday. Right, top, Schweitzer and his daughter, Rhena, in Lambaréné, 1963. Right: Dr. Schweitzer and members of his staff give out work assignments to workers at the jungle hospital.

*Below, left: Dr. Albert Schweitzer stops to talk to a patient during a tour
of the hospital in 1963. The doctor, nearing eighty-nine by this time, no
longer practiced medicine himself, but did actively direct the construction
of a new ward at the hospital. Below: The doctor works as his
cat, one of the many animals around the hospital, plays near him on the desk.*

At Monday morning sick call, outpatients and new patients wait in front of the dispensary on the main street of the hospital compound in Lambaréné.

81

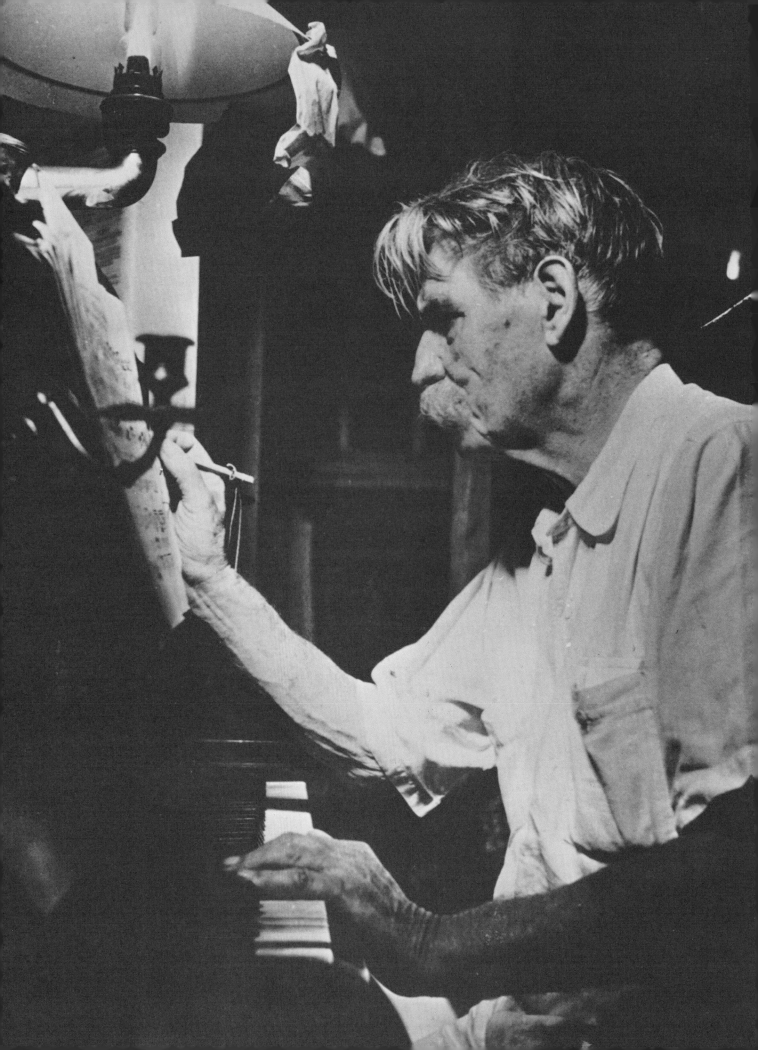

Opposite: Schweitzer composes and plays the lead-lined piano that had been presented to him many years before by the Paris Bach Society. Right: A German worker at the hospital buys bananas in a nearby village to supply part of the food for the hospital staff, the patients, and their families.

Dr. Schweitzer, nearing the end of his fiftieth year in Africa, strolls in the hospital compound with a few of the many animals he kept as pets.

(*text continued from page 71*)

In the summer of 1941, Mme. Schweitzer arrived at Lambaréné, safe and healthy, much to the doctor's delight. She had made her way to Portugese Angola by ship and then overland to Lambaréné. Mme. Schweitzer remained in Africa until after the war ended in September of 1945.

There were shortages and a few hard times during the war period, but the resourcefulness of Dr. Schweitzer prevailed and the hospital continued its fine work uninterrupted. Just when supplies were getting dangerously low, a large shipment of medical stores arrived from America. News also came that Rhena had married an old friend in Switzerland.

It was October of 1948 before Dr. Schweitzer managed to return to Europe. The hospital was now thriving and boasted 40 buildings, beds for 350 patients, and a staff of 20. But it required money to continue the work, and so the doctor returned to Europe to seek funds. He had another reason for wanting to return. He wanted to see for the first time the four grandchildren born during his absence.

In 1949, Schweitzer made his first and only trip to America. He was already well known in America, as Mme. Schweitzer had made two trips here on fund-raising tours before the war. The Albert Schweitzer Fellowship of America had been established in 1939. Now, ten years later, he made two speeches at Aspen, Colorado, commemorating the bicentenary of the birth of Goethe. With his fee, he purchased a large supply of the new American drug, promin diasone, which had proved effective against leprosy.

Returning to Africa in the fall of 1949, Schweitzer immediately began plans for a new leprosarium. A great amount of money was going to be needed, and he was gravely concerned about where it would come from. Then, in 1951, he was awarded the Peace Prize of the German Association of Publishers, which amounted to ten thousand marks. The leprosarium was a little nearer completion. In 1952 came the biggest prize of all—the Nobel Peace Prize, which amounted to some $33,000. Dr. Schweitzer was deeply honored by the award, but the satisfaction of knowing the leprosarium could now be completed was especially warming.

In 1955, Queen Elizabeth paid Dr. Schweitzer the highest honor the British Crown can bestow—the British Order of Merit. Only one other foreigner has ever received the medal and that was General Dwight D. Eisenhower for leading the Allies to victory over the Nazis.

In 1957, following a prolonged illness, Mme. Schweitzer passed away at Lambaréné. Her long years of toil and dedication at her husband's side were over. Dr. Schweitzer would now continue the work alone.

The remaining years of Albert Schweitzer's life were spent in the quiet jungles along the Ogowe River, with an occasional trip to Europe to reap more honors and acclaim. Gradually the giant frame became more and more stooped, the unruly mane of hair and bristling mustache a little whiter. Great men came to pay him honor and to view firsthand the modern hospital complex this almost legendary man had forged out of a jungle wilderness with forty years of dedication and hard labor.

On September 4, 1965, Dr. Albert Schweitzer died at the hospital at Lambaréné. The years of hardship and sacrifice are not forgotten. The great work at Lambaréné continues. And there beside the yellow waters of the Ogowe, Albert Schweitzer, boy of the Vosges, enemy of pain and suffering, lies quietly at last after ninety years of reverence for life.

On September 4, 1965, the long and productive life of Albert Schweitzer, philosopher, theologian, preacher, and doctor, came to an end. After his funeral (opposite, top) he was buried in Lambaréné (opposite, bottom).

Summary

Albert Schweitzer is almost unique in history. During his lifetime he became one of the most famous men in the world—and yet he never sought fame or glory. Millions of people the world over knew his name and praised his work and ideals, yet he came in contact with relatively few during his life. He did not lead great armies or nations and he held no high rank except in the hearts of his fellowmen. Yet he became a legend in his own time.

As with many great men, his background was simple and unpromising. The son of a poor Protestant minister, his childhood was uneventful in the quiet countryside of the Vosges Mountains. A child of the church, he found pleasure and beauty in all God's creations—the forests and streams, the clouds and the sky, and the animal life he encountered as a boy. At a very early age he developed an acute sensitivity to pain—any pain as experienced by any living creature. He became the avowed enemy of pain in every form.

His sense of beauty encompassed the world of music. Even as a young man he became recognized as one of the most accomplished organists in Europe.

Through sheer determination and willpower he developed an awesome capacity for work and study. He found a deep and profound happiness in every endeavor, in every accomplishment and, indeed, in life itself. He began to ask himself if he had the right to accept this happiness as a matter of course. At last he decided he did not. And then he found the key to his life. "Out of the depths of my feeling of happiness there grew up gradually within me an understanding of the saying of Jesus that we must not treat our lives as being for ourselves alone."

When he was twenty-one he made a vow. He would devote the next nine years to theology, science, and music. After that he decided he would "take a path of immediate service as man to my fellow man." He did not know at that time that his destiny lay along the banks of the Ogowe River in Africa.

For the last half-century of his life, Dr. Schweitzer spent most of his years administering to the primitive natives of Gabon in French Equatorial Africa. Dr. Schweitzer, the man, personally touched a few thousand persons at his modest jungle hospital. But Dr. Schweitzer, the symbol, touched the hearts of countless millions who heard of his dedication and work at Lambaréné.

Albert Schweitzer achieved his destiny as a symbol of man's finest relationship to his fellow man. By his example and devoted service to suffering humanity, Dr. Schweitzer tested the conscience of all men. And he gave to the world a philosophy—one by which he lived his life and which he felt expressed the hope and promise of civilization. He called it *Erfurcht vor dem Leben*—"Reverence for Life."

Bibliography

ANDERSON, ERICA. *Albert Schweitzer's Gift of Friendship*. New York: Harper & Row, 1964.

———. *The Schweitzer Album*. New York: Harper & Row, 1965.

———. *The World of Albert Schweitzer*. New York: Harper, 1955.

———. *The Hospital at Lambaréné*, documentary film.

BERRILL, JACQUELYN. *Albert Schweitzer, Man of Mercy*. New York: Dodd, 1956.

CLARK, HENRY. *The Ethical Mysticism of Albert Schweitzer*. Boston: Beacon, 1962.

COUSINS, NORMAN. *Dr. Schweitzer of Lambaréné*. New York: Harper, 1960.

FESCHOTTE, JACQUES. *Albert Schweitzer*. Boston: Beacon, 1955.

FRANCK, FREDERICK. *Days with Albert Schweitzer*. New York: Holt, 1959.

GOLLUMB, JOSEPH. *Albert Schweitzer, Genius in the Jungle*. New York: Vanguard, 1949.

HAGEDORN, HERMAN. *Prophet in the Wilderness*. New York: Macmillan, 1954.

JOY, CHARLES. *The Africa of Albert Schweitzer*. London: Black, 1958.

———. *The Music of Albert Schweitzer*. New York: Harper, 1951.

LIVINGSTONE, DAVID. *The Last Journals of David Livingstone*. New York: Harper.

MCKNIGHT, GERALD. *Verdict on Schweitzer, The Man Behind the Legend*. New York: John Day, 1964.

MANTON, JO. *The Story of Albert Schweitzer*. New York: Abelard, 1955.

MONTAGUE, JOSEPH FRANKLIN. *The Why of Albert Schweitzer*. New York: Hawthorn Books, Inc., 1965.

MOZLEY, E. N. *The Theology of Albert Schweitzer*. New York: Macmillan, 1951.

MURRY, JOHN M. *Love, Freedom and Society*. London: Cape, 1957.

OSTERGAARD-CHRISTENSEN, LAVRIDS. *At Work with Albert Schweitzer*. Boston: Beacon, 1962.

OXNAM, GARFIELD B. *Personalities in Social Reform*. New York: Abington-Cokesbury Press, 1950.

PAYNE, ROBERT. *The Three Worlds of Albert Schweitzer*. New York: Nelson, 1957.

PHILLIPS, HERBERT M. *Safari of Discovery*. New York: Twayne, 1958.

PICHT, WERNER. *The Life and Thought of Albert Schweitzer*. New York: Harper & Row, 1964.

PIERNAL, JEAN. *Albert Schweitzer, the Story of his Life*. New York: Philosophical Library, 1957.

RATTER, MAGNUS C. *Albert Schweitzer*. Boston: Beacon, 1950.

———. *Dr. Schweitzer: Ninety Years Wise*. London: Religious Education Press, 1964.

ROBACK, A. A. *Albert Schweitzer Jubilee Book*. Cambridge, Mass.: Science-Art Publications, 1945.

———. *In Albert Schweitzer's Realms*. London: Science-Art Publications, 1962.

SCHWEITZER, ALBERT. *African Notebook.* New York: Henry Holt, 1939.

——. *An Anthology.* Boston: Beacon, 1956.

——. *The Animal World of Albert Schweitzer.* Boston: Beacon, 1950

——. *Christianity and the Religions of the World.* New York: Macmillan, 1923.

——. *Civilization and Ethics.* London: Black, 1946.

——. *Goethe, Four Studies.* Boston: Beacon, 1949.

SCHWEITZER, ALBERT. *J. S. Bach.* London: Black, 1923.

——. *The Light Within Us.* New York: Philosophical Library, 1959.

——. *Memoirs of Childhood and Youth.* New York: Macmillan, 1948.

——. *The Mystery of the Kingdom of God.* New York: Macmillan, 1950.

——. *The Mysticism of Paul The Apostle.* New York: Holt, 1931.

——. *On the Edge of the Primeval Forest.* New York: Macmillan, 1948.

——. *Out of My Life and Thought.* New York: Holt, 1949.

——. *Paul and His Interpreters.* New York: Macmillan, 1951.

——. *Peace or Atomic War?* New York: Holt, 1958.

——. *Philosophy of Civilization.* New York: Macmillan, 1949.

——. *The Psychiatric Study of Jesus.* Boston: Beacon, 1948.

——. *Quest For the Historical Jesus.* New York: Macmillan, 1910.

——. *The Teaching of Reverence for Life.* New York: Holt, 1965.

——. *Eugen Munch, 1857–1898.* Mulhouse, Alsace: J. Brinkmann, 1898.

——. *Indian Thought and its Development.* New York: Henry Holt and Co., 1936.

——. *Music in the Life of Albert Schweitzer.* By Charles R. Joy, with selections from the writings of Dr. Schweitzer. New York: Harper & Bros.; Boston: The Beacon Press, 1951.

SCHWEITZER, ALBERT. *The Wit and Wisdom of Albert Schweitzer.* A book of epigrams compiled with an introduction by Charles R. Joy. Boston: The Beacon Press, 1949.

——. "Busy Days in Lambaréné." *The Christian Century,* Vol. LI (March 14, 1934), pp. 355-357.

——. "The Ethics of Reverence for Life." *Christendom,* Vol. I, No. 2 (Winter, 1936), pp. 225-239.

——. "Goethe, His Personality and His Work." In *Goethe and the Modern Age.* Edited by Arnold Bergstraesser. Chicago: Henry Regnery Co., 1950, pp. 95-110.

——. "Letter from Lambaréné." *The Living Age,* Vol. CCLV (Sept., 1938), pp. 70ff.

——. "The One-Talent People." *The Christian Herald,* Vol. LXII (Sept., 1949), p. 24.

——. "The Relations of the White and Colored Races." *The Contemporary Review,* Vol. CXXXIII, No. 745 (Jan., 1928), pp. 65-70.

——. "Religion and Modern Civilization." *The Christian Century,* Vol. LI, No. 47 (Nov. 21, 1934), pp. 1483-1484; No. 48 (Nov. 28, 1934), pp. 1519-1521.

——. "Return to Colmar." London: *Daily Mail,* Sept. 25, 1950.

——. "Sermon on Forgiveness." *The Christian World,* Nov. 1, 1934, p. 11.

——. "Sunday at Lambaréné." *The Christian Century,* Vol. XLVIII (March 18, 1931), pp. 540-541.

SCIPIO, CORNELIUS (psuedo.). "Is Schweitzer Dead?" *Atlantic Monthly,* August, 1966.

SEAVER, GEORGE. *Albert Schweitzer, a Vindication.* Boston: Beacon, 1951.

——. *Albert Schweitzer, The Man and His Mind.* New York: Harper, 1955.

SIMON, CHARLIE MAY. *All Men Are Brothers.* New York: Dutton, 1956.

SMITH, E. W. *African Ideas of God.* London: Edinburgh House Press, 1950.

WARD, HERBERT. *A Voice from the Congo.* London: William Hunemann, 1910.

Index